FIGHTER JETS

Valerie Bodden

CREATIVE EDUCATION

Published by Creative Education
P.O. Box 227, Mankato, Minnesota 56002
Creative Education is an imprint of The Creative Company
www.thecreativecompany.us

Design and production by Liddy Walseth
Art direction by Rita Marshall
Printed by Corporate Graphics in the United States of America

Photographs by Alamy (Yagil Henkin), Getty Images (Paul Bowen, Ed Darack, U.S. Navy/digital version by Science Faction), iStockphoto (Ugur Demir, Chris Downie, FotoVoyager, Andrew Howe, Mistikas, Naphtalina, Picmax, Lowell Sannes, Robert Simon, Thomas Sztanek), Shutterstock (Christopher Parypa)

Library of Congress Cataloging-in-Publication Data

Bodden, Valerie.
Fighter jets / by Valerie Bodden.
Includes bibliographical references and index.
Summary: A fundamental exploration of fighter jets, including their speed and maneuverability, history of development, cockpits and other features, and famous models from around the world.
ISBN 978-1-60818-126-1
1. Jet fighter planes—Juvenile literature. I. Title.
UG1242.F5B627 2011
623.74'64—dc22 2010054403

CPSIA: 030111 PO1447

First edition
2 4 6 8 9 7 5 3 1

BUILT for BATTLE

FIGHTER JETS

Valerie Bodden

TABLE OF contents

An airplane speeds through the sky. It zigs and zags to dodge MISSILES (MIS-sulz) from an enemy plane. It makes quick turns and even rolls upside down. This is a fighter jet!

A fighter jet is a small, fast airplane that carries weapons. Its main job is to shoot down enemy airplanes. Some fighter jets also shoot targets on the ground. The fastest fighter jets can zoom through the air at 1,900 miles (3,058 km) per hour!

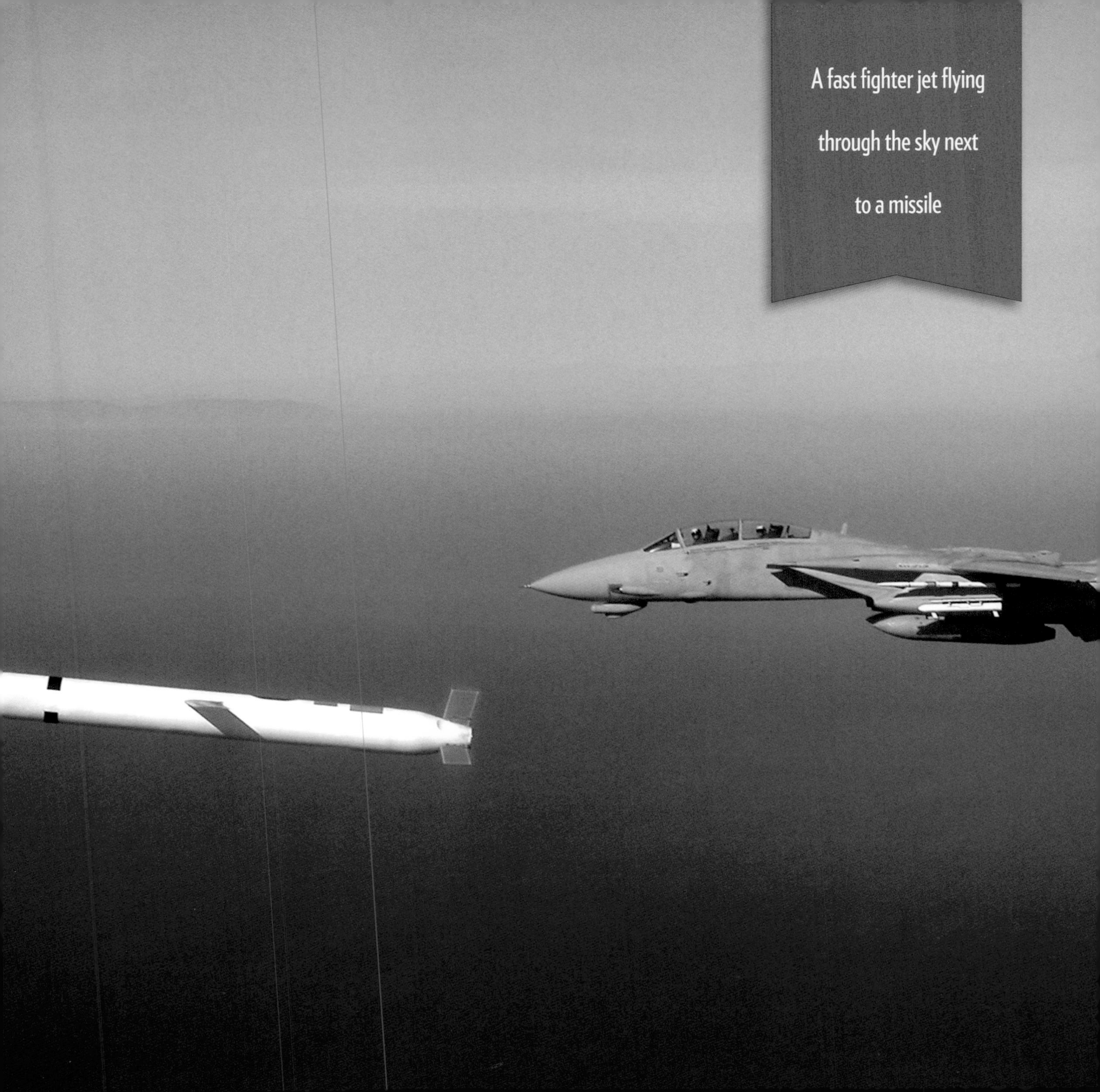

A fast fighter jet flying through the sky next to a missile

These fighter jets called
P-51 Mustangs were
used in the 1940s

Airplane pilots first fought against each other around 1914. The pilots shot guns at each other from the open COCKPITS of their planes. Later, faster planes with JET ENGINES were made. They had guns and other weapons built onto them.

★ Famous Fighter Jet ☆

Me 262 Schwalbe

COUNTRY
Germany

ENTERED SERVICE
1944

LENGTH
34.8 feet (10.6 m)

WINGSPAN
41 feet (12.5 m)

WEIGHT
4.2 tons (3.8 t)

FASTEST SPEED
540 miles (869 km) per hour

CREW
1

The Me 262 was the first
jet-engine-powered fighter airplane.
It could fly 100 miles (160 km)
per hour faster than other
fighter airplanes of the 1940s!

Today, most fighter jets are about 50 to 60 feet (15-18 m) long. From the tip of one wing to the tip of the other, they reach about 40 feet (12 m) or more. That is as long as a school bus.

A big, curved window covers the cockpit of a fighter jet. The window lets the pilot see all around and above the jet. The cockpit also has a control stick for steering the jet.

Brightly colored images on a jet cockpit's HUD screen

Fighter pilots do not look down at their controls when they are fighting another jet. Instead, they see all the information they need on a head-up display (HUD) screen. The HUD screen can be on the cockpit's window or on the pilot's helmet visor.

Fighter jets usually go into battle in groups. The pilots fly in FORMATION to protect each other. When they reach enemy airplanes, they shoot at them with big guns, missiles, and other weapons.

Fighter jets (top); a
pilot (bottom left); a
missile (bottom right)

F-22 Raptor

COUNTRY
United States
ENTERED SERVICE
2005
LENGTH
62 feet (18.9 m)
WINGSPAN
44.5 feet (13.6 m)
WEIGHT
21.7 tons (19.7 t)
FASTEST SPEED
1,600 miles (2,575 km) per hour
CREW
1

The F-22 Raptor is a stealth fighter.
That means that its shape makes
it hard for enemy RADAR to see.
It can attack other fighter jets or
targets on the ground.

If an enemy shoots at a fighter jet, the pilot quickly changes direction so that the jet does not get hit. The pilot's fancy flying keeps the fighter jet safe to fight another day!

23

GLOSSARY

cockpits—the parts of airplanes or helicopters where the pilot and other crew members sit

formation—the way a group of fighter jets is arranged in the air to protect one another

jet engines—machines that move an airplane forward by pulling air in through the front of the engine and pushing it out the back

missiles—exploding weapons that are pushed through the air by rockets to hit a target

radar—a system that uses radio waves and computers to find objects such as enemy airplanes

INDEX

READ MORE

Demarest, Chris. *Alpha, Bravo, Charlie: The Military Alphabet.* New York: Margaret K. McElderry Books, 2005.

Zobel, Derek. *F-22 Raptors.* Minneapolis: Torque Books, 2009.

WEB SITES

Fighter Jet Pictures http://fighterjetpics.webs.com/ See pictures of fighter jets and listen to the sounds their engines make.

Super Coloring: Military Coloring Pages http://www .supercoloring.com/pages/category/military/ Print and color pictures of all your favorite military machines.